HOW YOUR BODY WORKS

GROWTH AND DEVELOPMENT

CELLS AND DNA

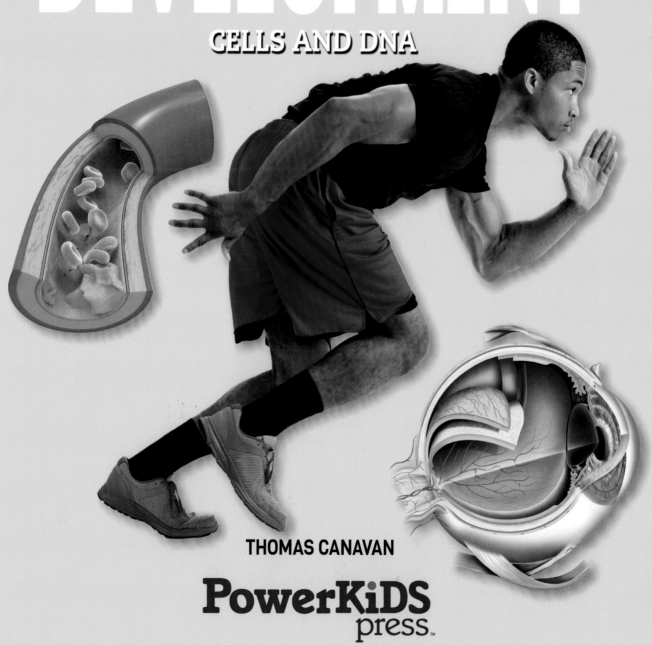

THOMAS CANAVAN

PowerKiDS press™

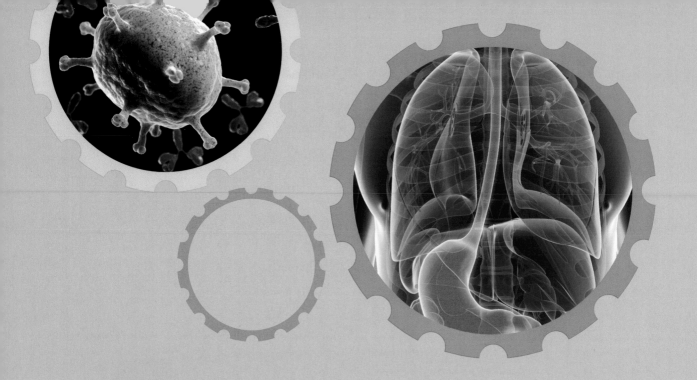

Published in 2016 by
The Rosen Publishing Group, Inc.
29 East 21st Street, New York, NY 10010

Cataloging-in-Publication Data
Canavan, Thomas.
Growth and development: cells and DNA / by Thomas Canavan.
p. cm. — (How your body works)
Includes index.
ISBN 978-1-4994-1228-4 (pbk.)
ISBN 978-1-4994-1252-9 (6 pack)
ISBN 978-1-4994-1241-3 (library binding)
1. DNA — Juvenile literature. 2. Heredity, Human — Juvenile literature.
3. Cells — Juvenile literature. I. Canavan, Thomas, 1956-. II. Title.
QP624.C218 2016
572.8'6—d23

Produced by Arcturus Publishing Limited,

Author: Thomas Canavan
Editors: Joe Harris, Joe Fullman, Nicola Barber and Sam Williams
Designer: Elaine Wilkinson
Original design concept and cover design: Notion Design

Picture Credits: All images courtesy of Shutterstock, apart from:
Lee Montgomery and Anne Sharp: back coverer, p30, p31.

Manufactured in the United States of America
CPSIA Compliance Information: Batch #WS15PK:
For Further Information contact Rosen Publishing, New York, New York at 1-800-237-9932

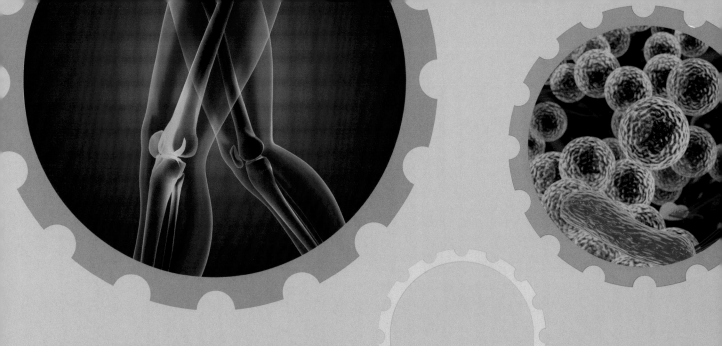

CONTENTS

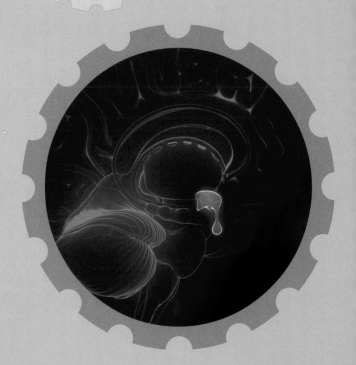

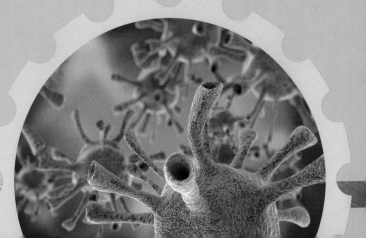

BUILDING A BODY

Your body is like a machine that's revving up and raring to go! But it's more amazing than any normal machine. Just think of all the incredible things your body can do: climbing trees, riding a bike, solving puzzles. It's remarkable!

Your body is special because it's totally different from anyone else's body. But at the same time, it's made from the same basic materials as everyone else. Tall or short, white or black – every one of us is a human being, and we're made of exactly the same ingredients. It's just how some of those ingredients are mixed around that makes us different.

Your body still hasn't finished growing and changing. Just think of all the things that you and your friends can do now – and what you can look forward to doing as you get older.

ALL IN THE MIX

Everything you see around you is made from a collection of basic materials called chemical elements. Your body is just the same. It's a wonderful mixture of different bits of matter that all add up to make . . . you!

IN YOUR ELEMENT

Scientists have identified 118 different basic materials or chemical elements. More than 99 percent of your body is entirely made from just six of these elements. Some of these elements work on their own and have special jobs. Others team up with other elements to build you up and keep your body super healthy.

Oxygen (61%)
This flows through your blood to give you energy.

Carbon (23%)
A building block for every cell in your body.

Hydrogen (10%)
Along with oxygen, hydrogen makes up the water that is found throughout your body.

Nitrogen (2.6%)
Important for growth and digestion.

Calcium (1.4%)
Helps build teeth and bones while looking after muscles.

Phosphorus (1%)
Like calcium, it helps build strong bones and teeth.

Trace elements (1%)

ADDED EXTRAS

The elements that make up the last 1 percent of your body are known as trace elements. A healthy diet allows your body to get all the trace elements it needs from food. For example, salt contains sodium and chlorine. Meat and fish contain iron. Potassium is found in fruits such as bananas. Sometimes, important trace elements are added to particular foods or drinks. Iodine is sometimes added to salt, and many breakfast cereals have added iron.

Salt is important for digestion and helps to balance the fluid in your body.

ACTIVITY

Iron carries oxygen all around your body and helps it to store and use oxygen.

Take a fortified breakfast cereal and check that it has added ingredients. Crush some cereal in a bowl and add water. Then, use a bar magnet and stir right to the bottom of the bowl. Now, look at the magnet. The black "dust" on it is iron.

Potassium helps to regulate how much water your body stores.

The average human body contains enough carbon to make

900

pencils!

BODY BUILDER

At the smallest level, your body is made up of atoms, which are tiny, nonliving pieces of elements such as iron or oxygen. Atoms join together with other atoms to form molecules. Molecules are not alive, either. It takes trillions of molecules organized in a very specific way to make the smallest living thing – a cell.

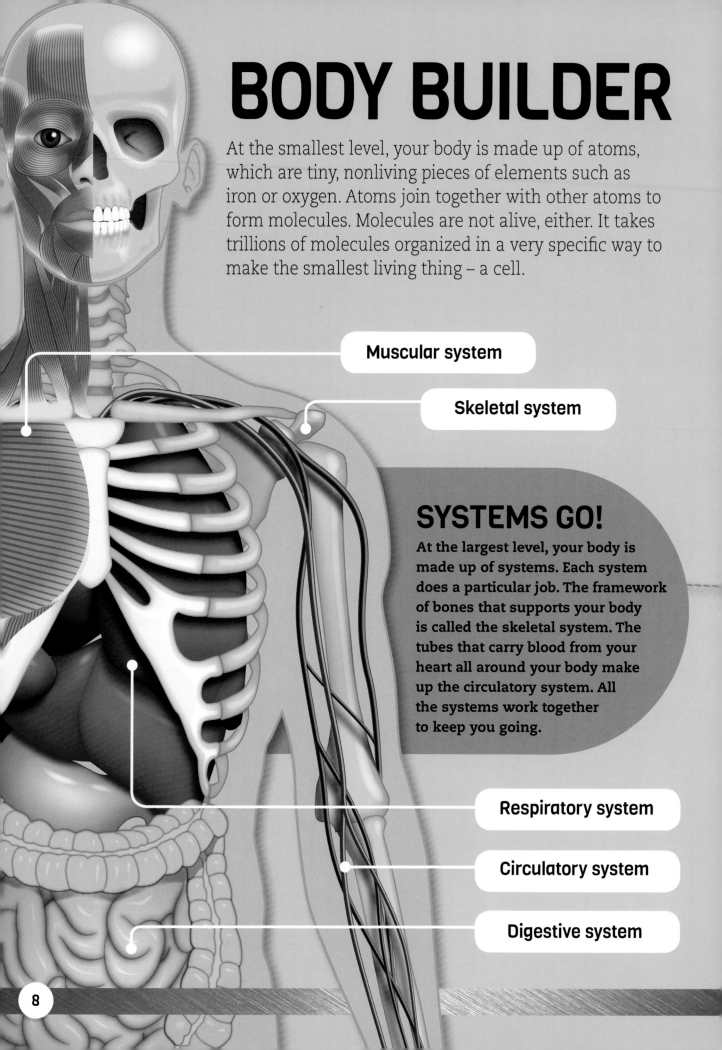

Muscular system

Skeletal system

SYSTEMS GO!

At the largest level, your body is made up of systems. Each system does a particular job. The framework of bones that supports your body is called the skeletal system. The tubes that carry blood from your heart all around your body make up the circulatory system. All the systems work together to keep you going.

Respiratory system

Circulatory system

Digestive system

PULLING TOGETHER

There are more than 200 types of cells in your body, and each has a different role. Cells of one type team up to make a tissue. It's the tissue that does the real work in your body! Muscle tissue is made of muscle cells, and is used for pushing and pulling. Other types of tissue do other important jobs.

GETTING ORGANIZED

Two or more types of tissue can combine to make organs. The organs are the major parts of the body, such as your eyes, your kidneys or your heart. Groups of organs are called systems.

WHAT MAKES YOU?

ATOMS
make up

MOLECULES
which make up

CELLS
which make up

TISSUES
which make up

ORGANS
which make up

SYSTEMS
which make up

YOUR BODY!

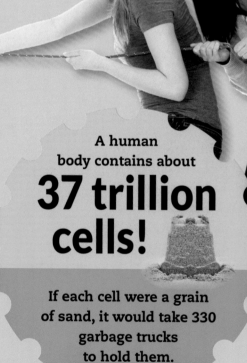

A human body contains about

37 trillion cells!

If each cell were a grain of sand, it would take 330 garbage trucks to hold them.

BACK TO BASICS

Your cells are constantly working. They take nutrients (important ingredients) from the food you eat and change those nutrients into energy. They do many different specialized jobs. For example, they fight disease and get rid of waste. They also store instructions about the future – how much you'll grow, whether you'll have curly or straight hair and what sort of features you'll pass on to your own children. Cells also have to reproduce, which adds even more to their incredible "to do" list!

Cells don't live as long as the person they make up. Some types die after a few days; others live up to a year.

MADE FOR THE TASK

Depending on where they are, and the job they have to do, cells have different shapes.

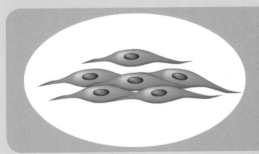

MUSCLE CELLS
These are long and tube-shaped. They can change shape by contracting – squeezing up to make themselves short. When many muscle cells contract at once, they move your body around.

NERVE CELLS
These are long and thin, and have branching end parts that allow them to carry messages to other cells. They connect to each other so that information can be sent quickly around your body.

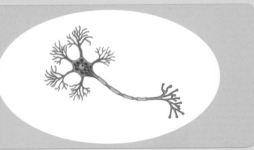

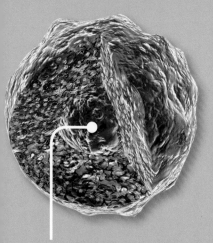

"MINI-ORGANS"

Each of your cells contains special parts called organelles. These carry out jobs to keep the cell active and useful. Some act like tiny factories, making useful molecules for the cell. Others transport molecules from one place to another. Some of the most important molecules are called proteins.

COMMAND HQ

The headquarters of the cell is called the nucleus. The nucleus contains an incredibly important type of protein, called DNA. This is the special code that instructs the cell about what to do and how to develop. So it is the nucleus that directs how the cell will grow – and when it's time to die.

Endoplasmic reticulum: helps the cell make and transport molecules.

Ribosomes: put together the proteins of the cell.

Centrioles: important for cell reproduction.

Nucleus: where the DNA is stored.

Golgi apparatus: sorts, organizes and sends molecules to the right places in the cell.

Plasma membrane: this protects the cell but lets helpful materials through.

Mitochondria: convert food energy into a form that the cell can use.

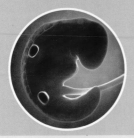

▲ At 4 weeks

You are a tiny blob no bigger than a poppy seed.

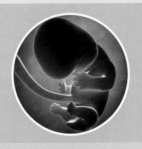

▲ At 8 weeks

Your heart begins to beat. Your body begins to take shape.

▲ At 16 weeks

You're about 4 inches (10 cm) long.

At 24 weeks

Hair begins to grow and you sleep and wake regularly.

At 36 weeks

You're running out of room to move and are almost ready to be born.

SMALL BEGINNINGS

Your body might have around 37 trillion cells now, but amazingly, you started out from just one cell! This cell divided into two and, over the course of about nine months, the cells kept dividing and dividing, again and again. As the cells divided, you changed from a tiny blob to a bigger blob and finally to a fully formed, small human being.

IN THE WOMB

All of this growing happened inside your mother's womb, or uterus, for about nine months before you were ready to be born. During that time your organs developed and you began to look more and more human. Being inside meant that you relied on your mother for oxygen and food, which came from an organ called the placenta through the umbilical cord – a tube that went into your stomach.

A mother-to-be can feel the baby inside her kicking from as early as four months into the pregnancy.

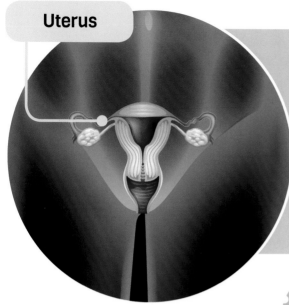

Uterus

BEFORE YOU BEGAN

Every month, an egg cell the size of a small pinhead is released inside your mother's uterus. This egg is ready to be fertilized, which means that it can combine with a sperm cell from your father. However, if no sperm cell is there to combine with it, the egg cell will be washed away.

RACE FOR THE EGG

About nine months before you were born, an incredible race took place – 300 million sperm cells, produced by your father, swam their way through special tubes to reach your mother's single egg cell. Only a few hundred of those made it to the egg. And only one of those cells actually broke through the cell membrane – the protective coating of the egg cell. Together your father's sperm and your mother's egg formed a single cell known as the fertilized egg cell.

NINE MONTHS

The fertilized egg cell grew and divided again and again . . . leading to your nine months developing inside your mother's uterus. We humans are complicated creatures, so we need to develop over a long time before we're ready to be born. But some creatures take even longer – elephants wait two years before they are born!

EGG MEETS SPERM

First, sperm cells enter the uterus.

Only around 200 sperm reach the single egg cell.

One sperm breaks through the cell membrane.

The sperm nucleus merges with the egg nucleus.

BRAND NEW YOU

Imagine spending nine months inside the same room, when that room seems to be getting smaller and smaller as you get bigger and bigger. That's what it's like when you're ready to be born. Things have become uncomfortable for you – and for your mother. You don't need to be inside there anymore, so it's time to see the outside world. It's your birthday!

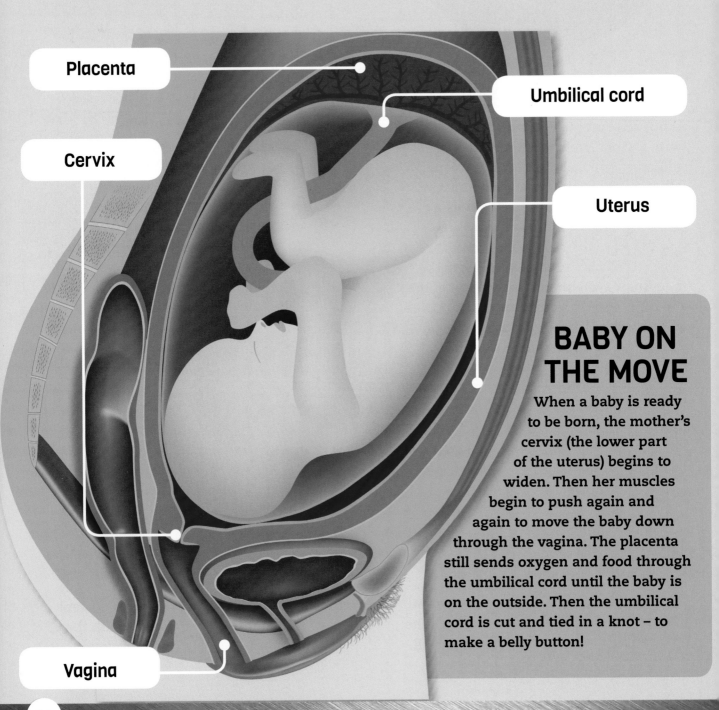

Placenta

Umbilical cord

Cervix

Uterus

Vagina

BABY ON THE MOVE

When a baby is ready to be born, the mother's cervix (the lower part of the uterus) begins to widen. Then her muscles begin to push again and again to move the baby down through the vagina. The placenta still sends oxygen and food through the umbilical cord until the baby is on the outside. Then the umbilical cord is cut and tied in a knot – to make a belly button!

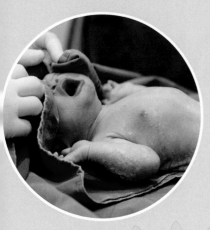

HAPPY BIRTHDAY!

The first sound you made was a loud cry. That wasn't because you were scared or unhappy. It was to try out your mouth, nose, and lungs for breathing. For the past nine months, the umbilical cord has been doing that for you.

MOTHER'S MILK

Soon after being born, you would have been given your first feed, either from your mother's breast or from a bottle. Newborn babies cannot see very well, but they quickly learn to recognize their mother's smell, and find cuddling and feeding comforting. You would have been given all the food you needed through liquids until you were about six months old.

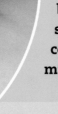

A NEW WORLD

Can you imagine experiencing everything for the first time? At first, the world would have been a confusing place to you. It takes babies a month or two before they can focus their eyes. Many scientists believe that babies' senses are confused at first – for example, they might "hear" pictures, or "see" music.

GROWING UP

You began growing the moment that your father's sperm fertilized your mother's egg. You're still growing now, and will continue to grow until you are about 18 or 19 years old. You go through lots of different stages of development before you become an adult. Then, as you head toward the middle of your life, you begin to notice signs that you're getting older.

JOURNEY OF LIFE

As a child, you become aware of your body, and how the muscles all work together. When you're six months old, just being able to sit up is a big deal. Less than two years later, you're able to pedal a tricycle. You reach your full height by the time you're 20 years old. By your forties you are what is called "middle-aged." Then, you reach old age once you are around 75 years old.

2 years old
Confident on your feet

8 years old
Growing about 2 inches (5 cm) in a year

14 years old
Reaching puberty

25 years old
Peak physical condition

45 years old
"Middle age"

75 years old
Old age

ON YOUR FEET!

You probably took your first steps when you were around a year old. You may have crawled first, then tried to stand up by holding on to things around you. By trial and error you learned what makes you trip or fall.

BIG CHANGES

At about 12 years old, you hit a big change called puberty. This is when children begin the change into adults. You're still growing, but your body changes shape a little as you begin to resemble an adult. It's not just how you look that changes either. Girls' voices become a little deeper and boys' voices become much deeper.

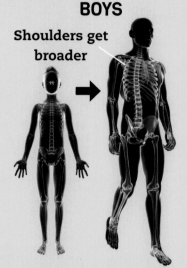

BOYS

Shoulders get broader

Body becomes more hairy

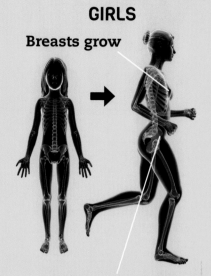

GIRLS

Breasts grow

Hips become wider

During the day, while you're standing up, the force of gravity pulls you down. So, each morning you wake up taller than when you went to sleep.

THE BALD TRUTH

One of the biggest clues that someone is reaching middle age is on the top of their head. Most men and women begin to get some silvery hairs, or maybe all of their hair turns that shade. Many men also lose some of their hair, usually from the front and top of their head.

SLOWING DOWN

Even the healthiest people begin to slow down as they enter old age. Their bodies can't recover from injury as well as before. Moving around takes more time because their muscles and bones aren't as strong.

YOU ARE UNIQUE

There are seven billion people alive in the world, but not a single one of them is exactly like you. Your body is different from anybody else's. That's just as well, because being able to prove who you are is important. Information about your unique body is called "biometric" information. It can be used in all sorts of ways.

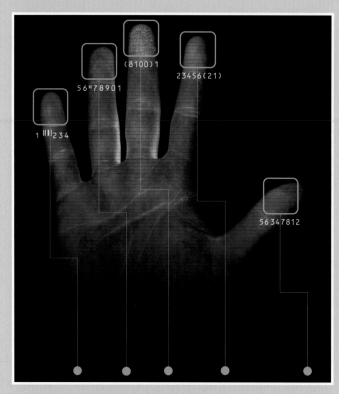

People can be identified from their fingerprints.

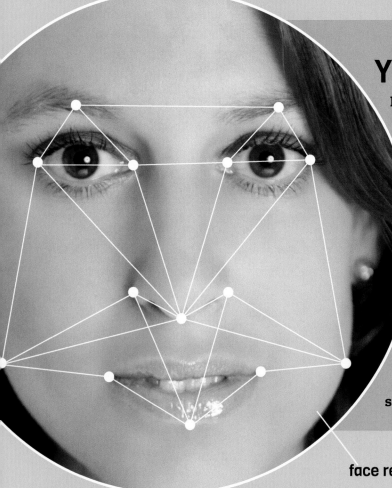

face recognition

YOUR ID, PLEASE?

Each year, large organizations find new ways to check people's identities. These checks are ways of stopping people from pretending they're you. A hundred years ago, a bank clerk would probably rely on recognizing your face if you wanted to take some money out of your account. Today, things are more advanced. Biometric identification can check different parts of your body, such as your hands and fingerprints (shown above) or face, with a camera or scanner to make sure it's really you. This kind of technology is even built into some modern phones.

SIGN ON THE DOTTED LINE

Some specialists are able to identify people by looking carefully at their handwriting. Is the writing big or small? Is it slanted or upright? Does the letter T look funny? Even if you try and disguise your writing, these experts believe they can identify you.

Loop   **Arch**   **Whorl**

WHORL LOT OF TROUBLE

Most people know that the police can check fingerprints to identify people. When you touch just about anything, you leave a print – even if you can't see it. That print is made by the patterns of little lines on each of your fingers. No two people have the same pattern of loops, whorls (spirals), and arches on their fingers.

Every person has a unique tongue print too!

⚇ ACTIVITY

You can "dust" a crime scene for prints! Put some cocoa powder into a cup. Dip a dry paintbrush into the powder and "dust" an area where there are fingerprints. Gently blow on the surface. Most of the powder will blow away, but some will stick to the grease of the fingerprints. Use a magnifying glass to find out: who did it?

A CODE FOR LIFE

Each of your body's trillions of cells contains a code. It's known as DNA, which is short for deoxyribonucleic acid. The "nucleic" in the middle of that big word tells you that the code is contained in the nucleus of each cell. This DNA code, or blueprint, guides the way cells grow, develop, and behave.

A TWIST OF FATE

DNA is a long, twisting molecule that is made up of four basic chemical building blocks – adenine, thymine, cytosine, and guanine. These form pairs inside the DNA. Each pair is like one rung of a long ladder, with a backbone holding those "rungs" in place. Although there are only four of these chemicals, they can be arranged to make many different combinations.

A gene is a length of DNA. Each cell in your body contains about 25,000 to 35,000 genes. These carry the information that makes you who you are. About 99.9 percent of the DNA of every person on the planet is exactly the same. It's the remaining 0.1 percent that makes each of us unique.

Because of the information in DNA, most people look a little like their parents. But not always!

IT'S IN THE GENES

Genes passed on to you from your parents determine many of your characteristics, known as traits. Inherited traits are ones you were born with and which you may pass on to your own children. They include whether you have blue or brown eyes. In fact, a scientist could look at your genes when you were a week old and have an idea about whether you will grow up to be tall or short, or whether you are likely to be good at sports or a talented artist.

NEW GENES

Sometimes, faulty genes can be passed on from parents to children, and can cause disease. Medical scientists are beginning to use "gene therapy" to prevent or treat some inherited diseases. One method involves replacing faulty genes with healthy ones.

DOUBLE TAKE

Have you ever wondered why identical twins are identical? It's because they've inherited exactly the same DNA. So if one of them has blonde hair, the other one will. And if one of them has lots of freckles, the twin will also be covered in freckles. Unless you're an identical twin, your DNA is different from everyone else who has ever lived.

ALL PART OF THE FAMILY

As a human, you are a type of animal, and that means that you are related to other animals. You may not be covered in fur or scales, but you have a lot in common with many other creatures, especially apes.

FAMILY PORTRAIT

You're part of a large group of animals known as mammals. Like other mammals, including cats, elephants, and mice, you have hair. Also, you didn't hatch from an egg and you drank your mother's milk (or similar milk) when you were a baby.

NOT SO DIFFERENT

Your body shares its basic structure with other mammals. You have exactly the same organ systems as a dog, though your brain or heart may not be the same shape or size. A giraffe may have a long neck, but it has just the same number of neck bones as a human.

OUR CLOSEST RELATIVES

Some mammals are so closely related that they share more than 98 percent of their DNA with us. They are the four types of great apes – gorillas, orangutans, chimpanzees, and bonobos.

Some scientists call humans "the third chimpanzee" because two types of chimpanzee – the common chimpanzee and the bonobo – are so closely related to humans.

98.4 percent

of a human's genes are identical to chimp genes.

WALKING TALL

Not everything about your body is the same as other apes, though. Walk a few steps and clap your hands at the same time. Easy – right? For humans, yes, but not for other apes. Chimpanzees and gorillas are on all fours a lot of the time. As a human, your bones are organized in a way that makes it easy for you to stand up.

DID YOU KNOW?

A BABY IS AS STRONG (FOR ITS SIZE!) AS AN OX

A newborn baby has a surprisingly strong grasp, which scientists call a "palmar grasp." Using this grasp, a baby could support its weight briefly – for maybe a few seconds – by hanging one-handed from a bar. That's the same strength as an ox pulling a wagon as heavy as itself.

YOU SHARE MORE THAN HALF OF YOUR DNA WITH A BANANA

All living things have DNA. Much of it – for example, the DNA that tells cells to get food or to reproduce – is shared by most organisms. You might not be "related" to a banana, but like a banana you grow, fight illness, and have parents.

TWO TWIN GIRLS WERE BORN 87 DAYS APART

Irish mother-to-be, Maria Jones-Elliott, knew she was expecting twins. But just over halfway through her pregnancy, she started to feel unwell and went into labor – 16 weeks too early. When the first twin, Amy, was born she weighed just 19 oz (539 g) and was rushed straight to intensive care (a ward for very ill patients). Then, incredibly, Maria's uterus closed up. Amy's twin sister, Katie, was born safely 87 days later, and the twins were reunited.

BABIES BLINK FAR LESS OFTEN THAN ADULTS

Don't try to play the blinking game with a baby! Infants blink only once or twice a minute while adults blink 10 to 15 times a minute. Scientists have come up with two theories to explain this. We know that blinking helps keep eyes moist and washes out dust and dirt. But because babies sleep so much, their eyes are probably less dry in the first place. Another theory is that while babies' eyes are still developing, they need to stay open as long as possible to take in all the information from the world around them.

MARK TWAIN PREDICTED THE USE OF FINGERPRINTS FOR CRIME-FIGHTING

The US author Mark Twain published his story "Life on the Mississippi" in 1883. It featured a murderer convicted because of fingerprint evidence – nine years before the first real-life investigation using fingerprints.

YOU HAVE A SMALL AMOUNT OF GOLD INSIDE YOUR BODY

In addition to oxygen, calcium and all the elements that keep you healthy, your body contains traces of other elements. Tiny amounts of gold are found in every human, mostly in blood. But you'd need about 40,000 people to get enough to make a gold coin!

WHY ARE WOMEN (USUALLY) SMALLER THAN MEN?

It's easier to understand this question if you remember that human beings are animals. And all animals – whether they're tigers, butterflies, or humans – need to reproduce. They can only do that if their bodies are mature, or physically prepared for the job. Scientists think that females mature earlier than males so that they have more years to produce babies. Maturing earlier means putting the brakes on growing. Going way back to our earliest ancestors, it's likely that women who matured earlier – even if they were still small – got to mate earlier.

DO ALL BABIES HAVE BLUE EYES?

Whether your eyes are brown, green, or blue depends on your parents – the color of your eyes is one of the many things you inherit from them. But no matter how your eyes look now, they were probably blue right after you were born. That's because there wasn't yet very much melanin, the substance that darkens skin, hair, and other body tissues, in your eyes. Without melanin, eyes look blue. Some people never have much melanin added, and their eyes remain blue. These people tend also tend to have lighter skin, for the same reason. Humans aren't the only animals to have blue-eyed babies – take a look at very young kittens once their eyes open.

WHY DO SOME PEOPLE HAVE INNIES AND OTHER PEOPLE HAVE OUTIES?

Most people can put the end of their finger into their belly button (an "innie"), but some people have a belly button that sticks out a little (an "outie'). Whether you have an innie or an outie depends on what happened before you were born. The belly button is a scar left from the umbilical cord, which carried oxygen and food from your mother while you were inside the womb. In some babies the skin grows out a little bit to join the umbilical cord. That bit of skin becomes an "outie" when the umbilical cord drops off after birth. If the skin didn't grow out in the first place, it's tucked inside, and you have an "innie."

WHY DO SOME TWINS LOOK IDENTICAL AND OTHERS LOOK DIFFERENT?

Sometimes – within 12 days of being fertilized – a mother's egg divides. Each of the halves goes on to develop into a separate baby. Those babies have identical genes, which means that they become identical twins, and they look alike. Fraternal (nonidentical) twins grow from two different eggs. These fertilized eggs develop into separate babies. They are (usually) born together, but they have different genes, so they do not look exactly the same.

SYSTEMS OF THE BODY

Skeletal system

The skeletal system supports and protects your body.

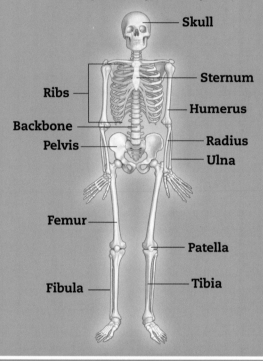

- Skull
- Sternum
- Ribs
- Humerus
- Backbone
- Radius
- Pelvis
- Ulna
- Femur
- Patella
- Fibula
- Tibia

Muscular system

The muscular system moves your body.

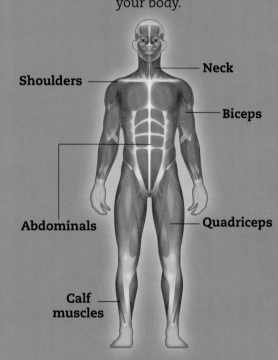

- Neck
- Shoulders
- Biceps
- Abdominals
- Quadriceps
- Calf muscles

Circulatory system

The circulatory system moves blood around your body.

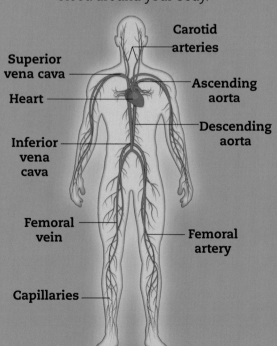

- Carotid arteries
- Superior vena cava
- Ascending aorta
- Heart
- Descending aorta
- Inferior vena cava
- Femoral vein
- Femoral artery
- Capillaries

Respiratory system

The respiratory system controls your breathing.

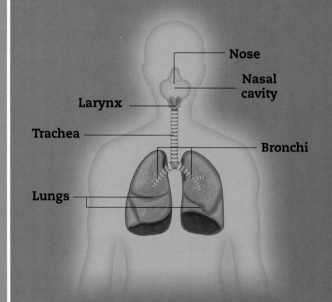

- Nose
- Nasal cavity
- Larynx
- Trachea
- Bronchi
- Lungs

This is your quick reference guide to the main systems of the body: skeletal, muscular, respiratory, circulatory, digestive, nervous, endocrine, and lymphatic.

Digestive system

The digestive system takes food in and out of your body.

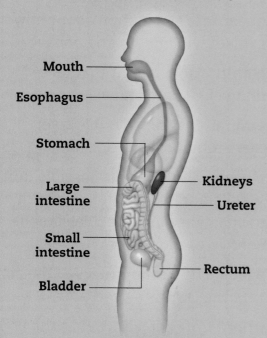

Mouth
Esophagus
Stomach
Large intestine
Small intestine
Bladder
Kidneys
Ureter
Rectum

Nervous system

The nervous system carries messages around your body and controls everything you do.

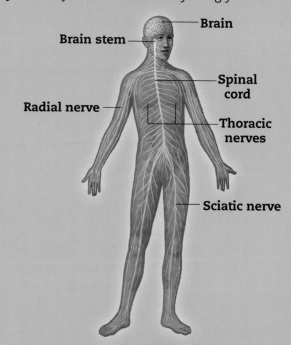

Brain
Brain stem
Spinal cord
Radial nerve
Thoracic nerves
Sciatic nerve

Endocrine system

The endocrine system produces hormones and controls your growth and mood.

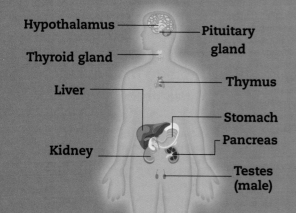

Hypothalamus
Thyroid gland
Liver
Kidney
Pituitary gland
Thymus
Stomach
Pancreas
Testes (male)

Ovaries (female)

Lymphatic system

The lymphatic system fights off germs and helps keep your body healthy.

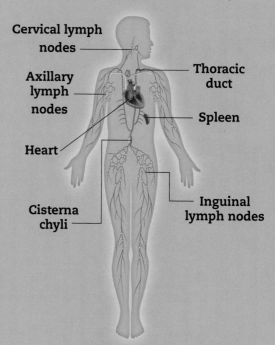

Cervical lymph nodes
Axillary lymph nodes
Heart
Cisterna chyli
Thoracic duct
Spleen
Inguinal lymph nodes

GLOSSARY

atom The smallest possible particle of a chemical element.

biometric Describes the science of measuring human characteristics and traits.

cell The basic unit of plants and animals. Each cell has a central control, or nucleus, and is surrounded by a thin membrane.

cervix The lower part of the uterus.

DNA Short for **deoxyribonucleic acid**, the chemical ingredient that forms genes. Parents pass on copied parts of their DNA to their children so that some of their traits (like height and hair type) are also passed on.

egg cell The female reproductive cell.

element A substance that cannot be broken down into simpler substances.

energy The power to be active and perform jobs.

gene A combination of chemicals that carries information about how an organism will appear and behave.

melanin The pigment that gives human skin, hair, and eyes their color.

membrane A thin, flexible layer of tissue around organs or cells.

molecule The smallest possible unit of a substance that still behaves like that substance. A molecule is made up of two or more atoms.

nucleus The headquarters of the cell where the DNA is stored.

nutrient Any substance that the body needs for energy or growth.

organ A collection of cells that work together to perform a specific function.

organelle Part of a cell that does one particular job.

placenta An organ that is attached to the inside of the uterus, which feeds the developing baby inside the womb.

plasma The fluid that carries the different blood cells through the body.

protein One of the most important of all molecules in the body, protein is needed to strengthen and replace tissue in the body. Muscles and many organs are made of protein.

puberty The time during the teenage years when a child's body matures into an adult body capable of reproduction.

sperm A male reproductive cell that combines with a female's egg to produce a new baby.

tissue A collection of cells that look the same and have a similar job to do in your body.

trace element Any chemical element required by living organisms in minute amounts.

trait A characteristic.

umbilical cord The tube that connects a baby in the womb to its mother, carrying oxygen and nutrients to the baby from the placenta, and waste products from the baby to the placenta.

uterus (womb) The organ in the female reproductive system in which a baby develops.

whorl A spiral pattern.

FURTHER READING

Body Works by Anna Claybourne (QED Publishing, 2014)

Complete Book of the Human Body by Anna Claybourne (Usborne Books, 2013)

Everything You Need to Know about the Human Body by Patricia MacNair (Kingfisher, 2011)

Eyewitness: Human Body by Richard Walker (Dorling Kindersley, 2014)

Horrible Science: Body Owner's Handbook by Nick Arnold (Scholastic Press, 2014)

How Your Body Works: Getting Energy by Philip Morgan (Franklin Watts, 2011)

Human Body A Children's Encyclopedia (Dorling Kindersley, 2012)

Mind Webs: Human Body by Anna Claybourne (Wayland, 2014)

Project Science: Human Body by Sally Hewitt (Franklin Watts, 2012)

Your Body for Life: From Birth to Old Age by Anne Rooney (Raintree, 2013)

INDEX